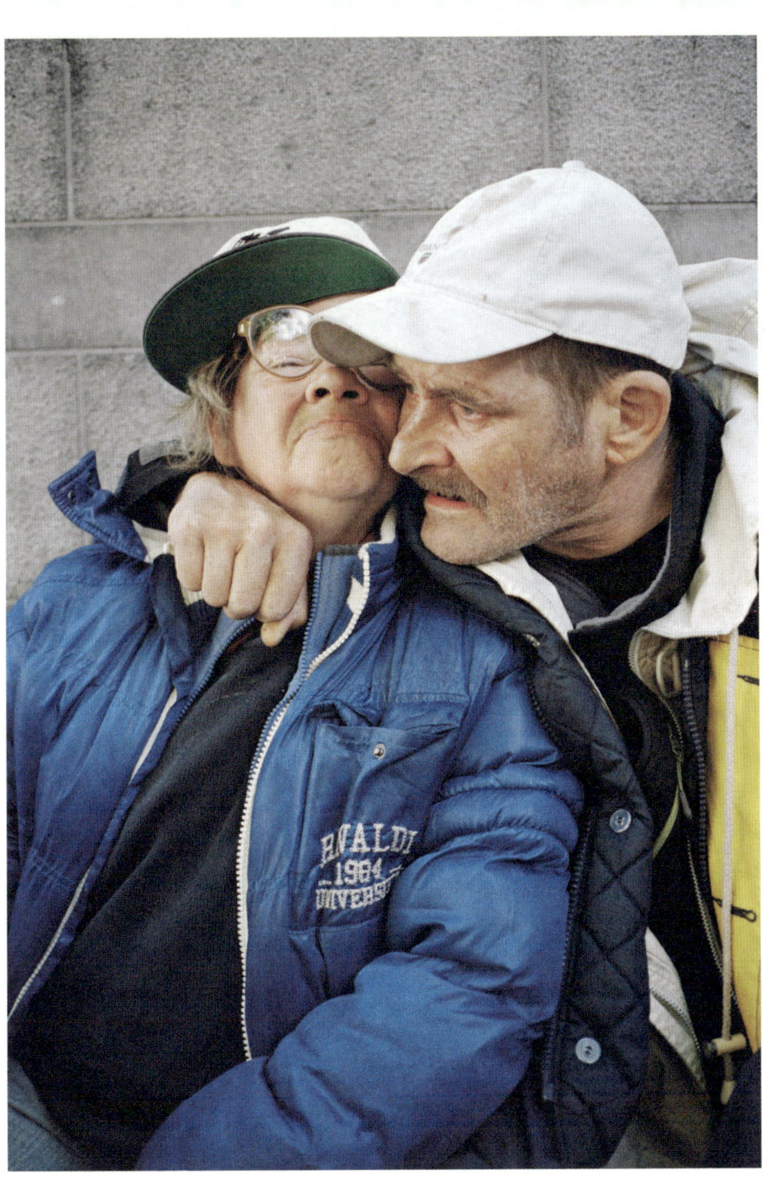

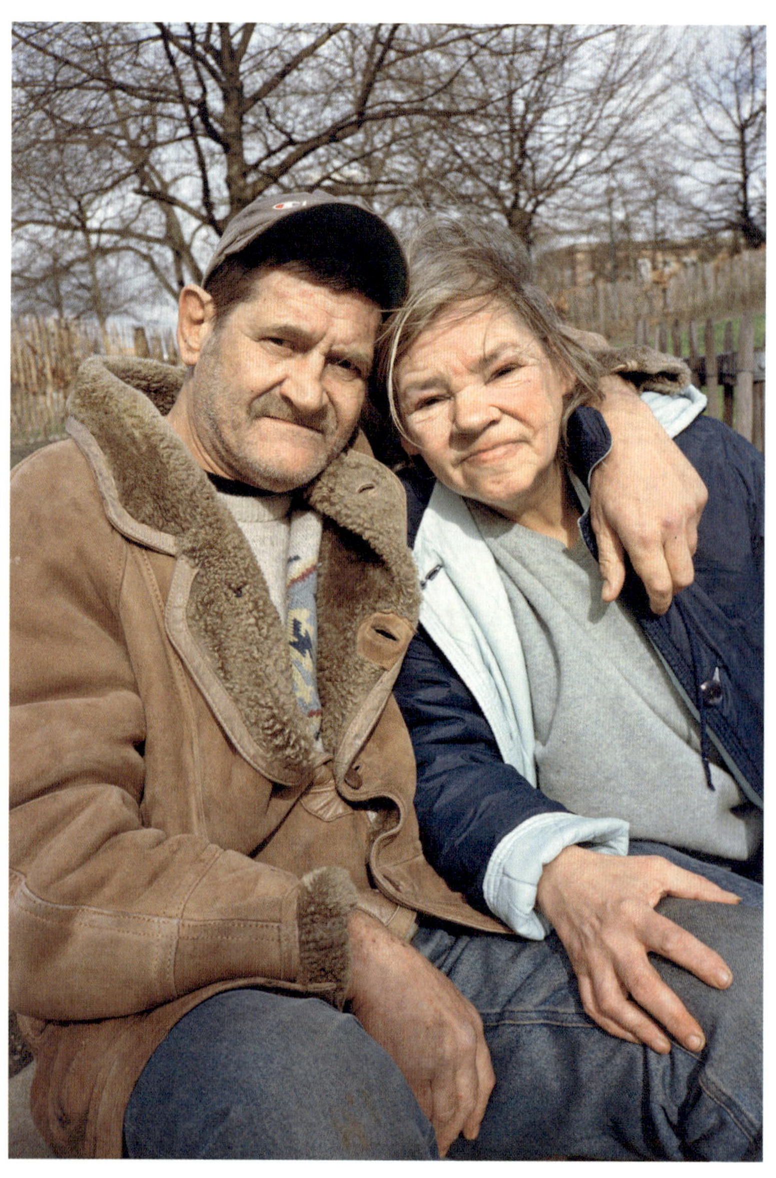

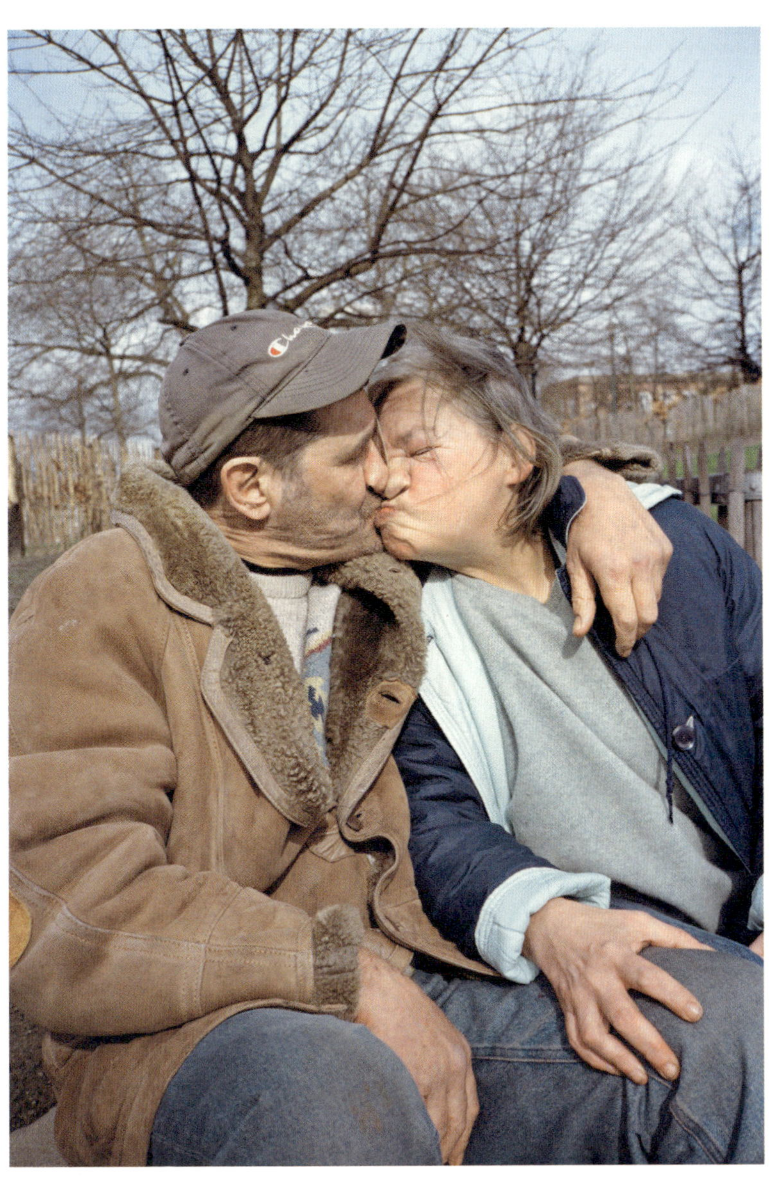

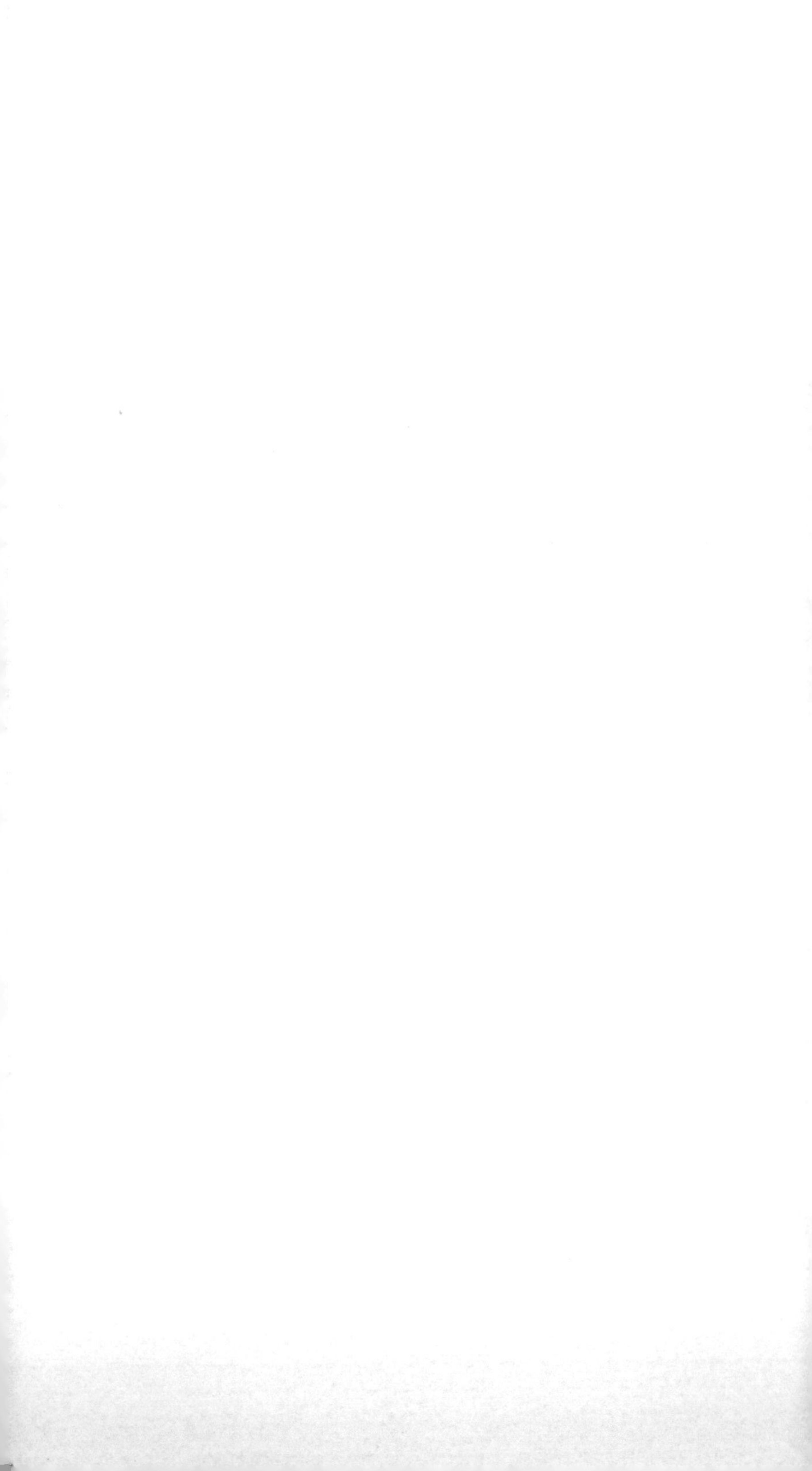

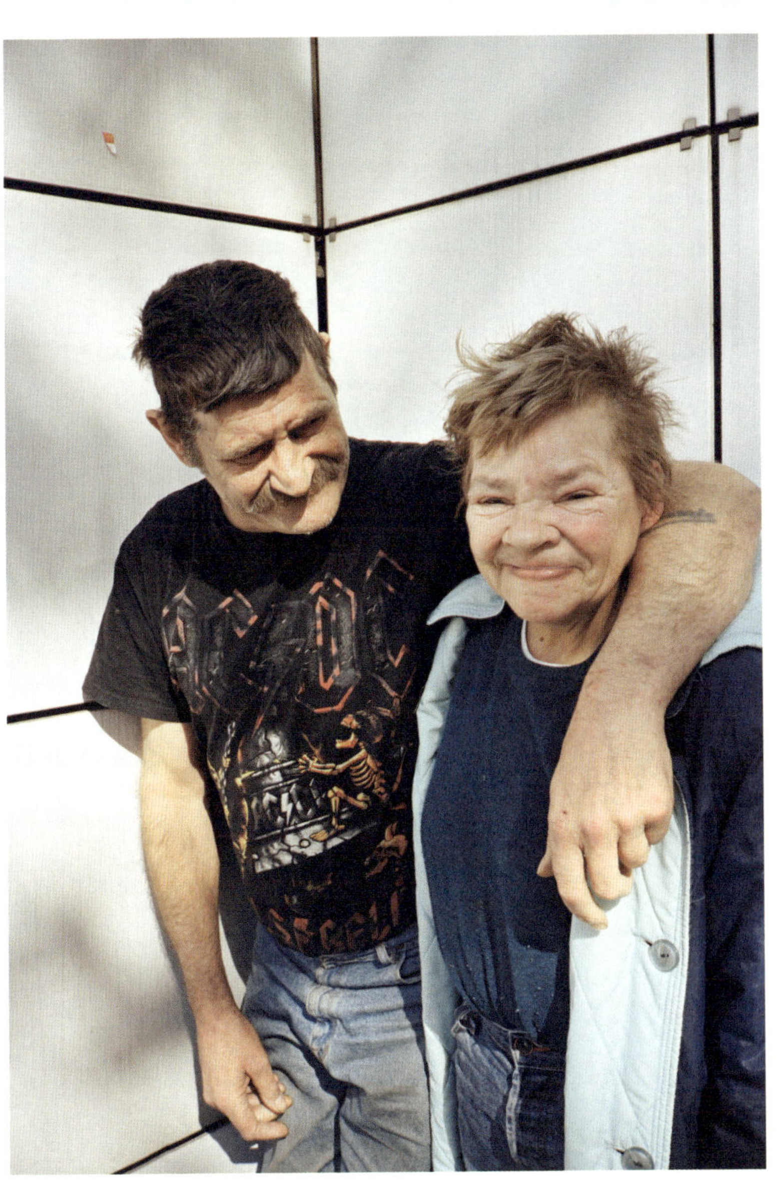

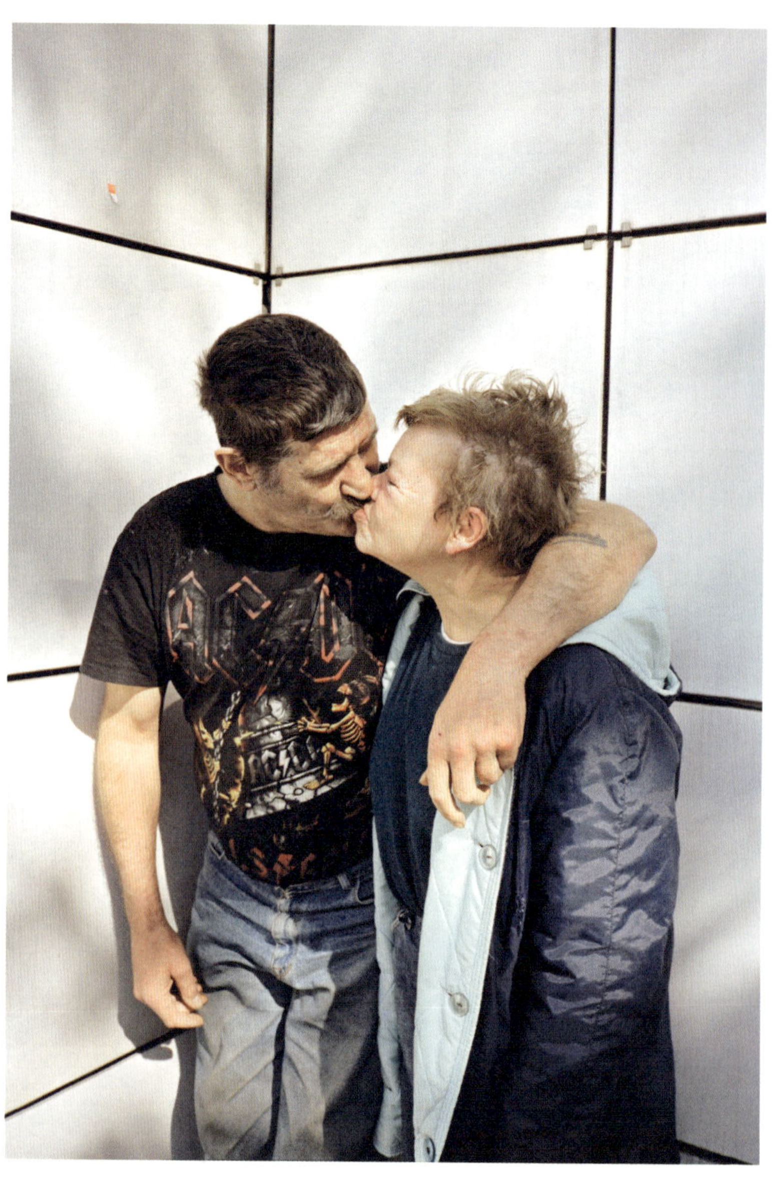
AC/DC
AC/DC

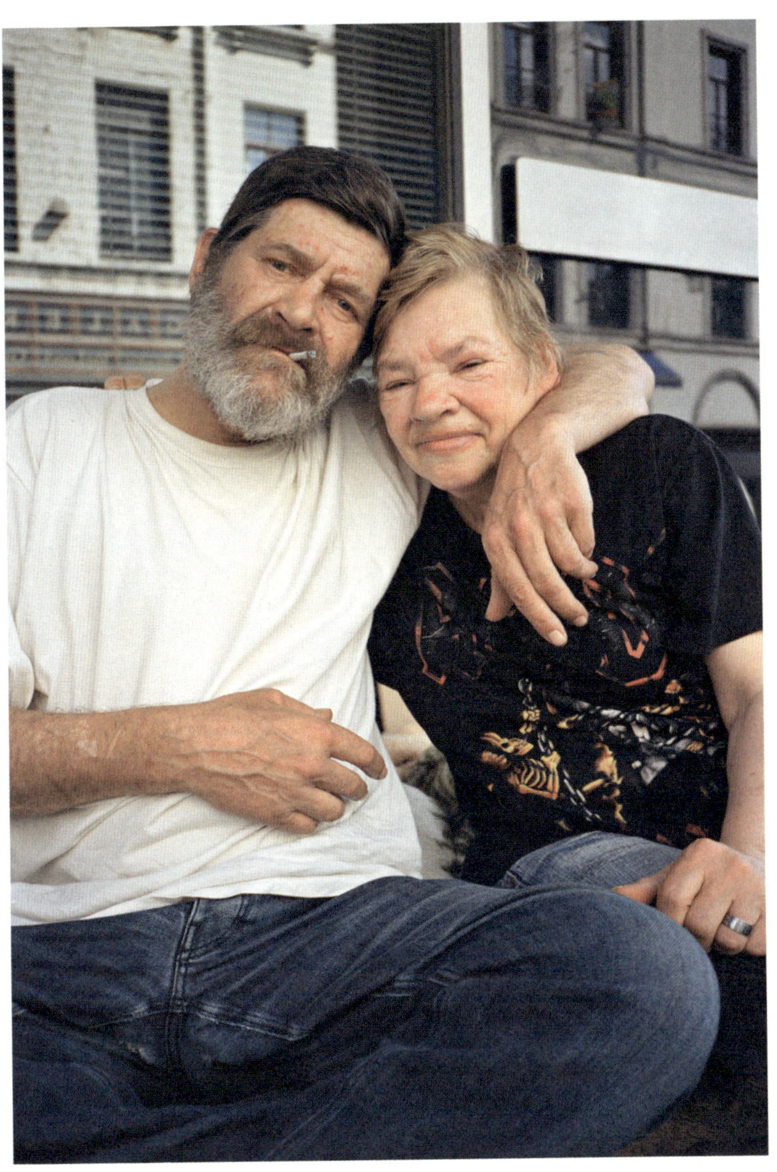

8/9

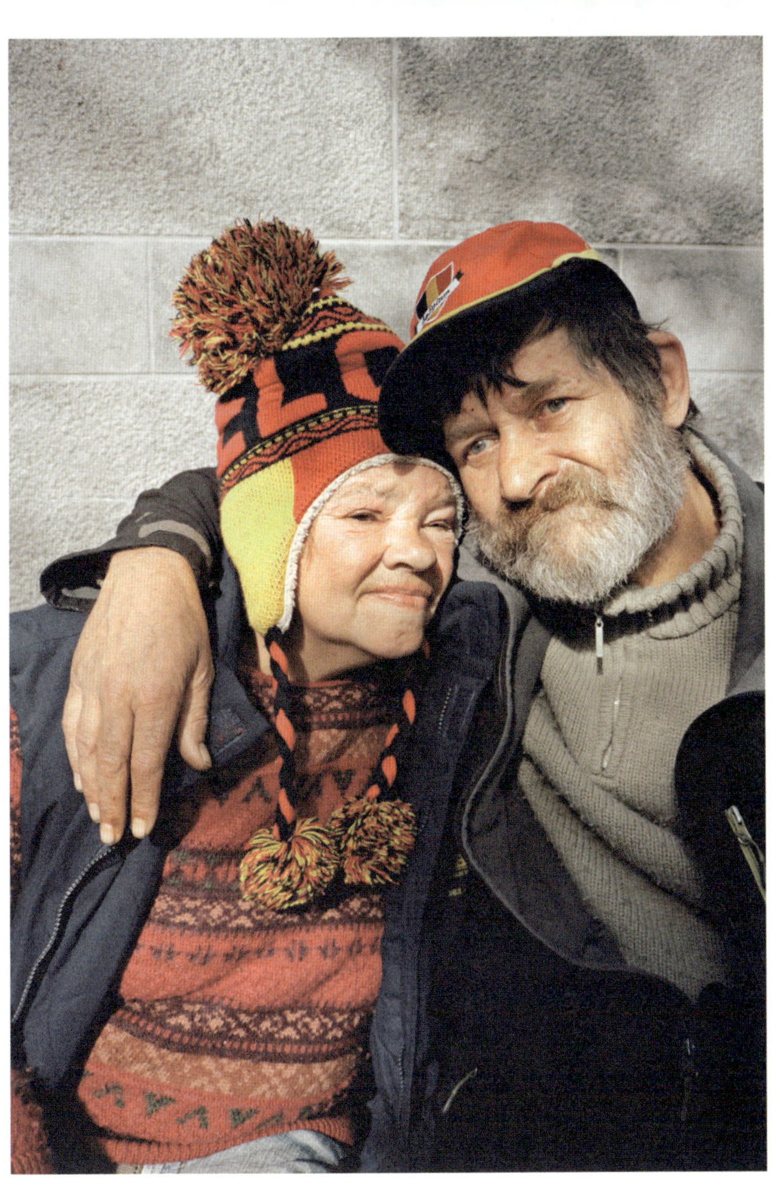

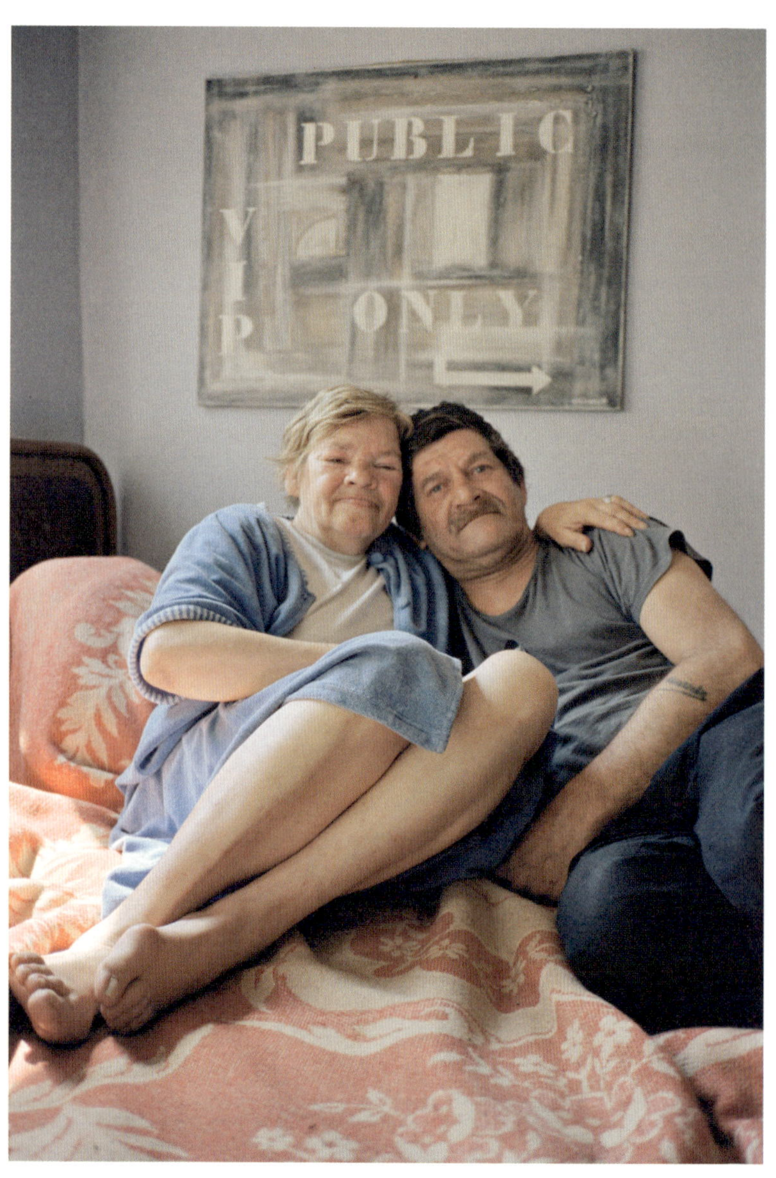
PUBLIC
VIP
ONLY

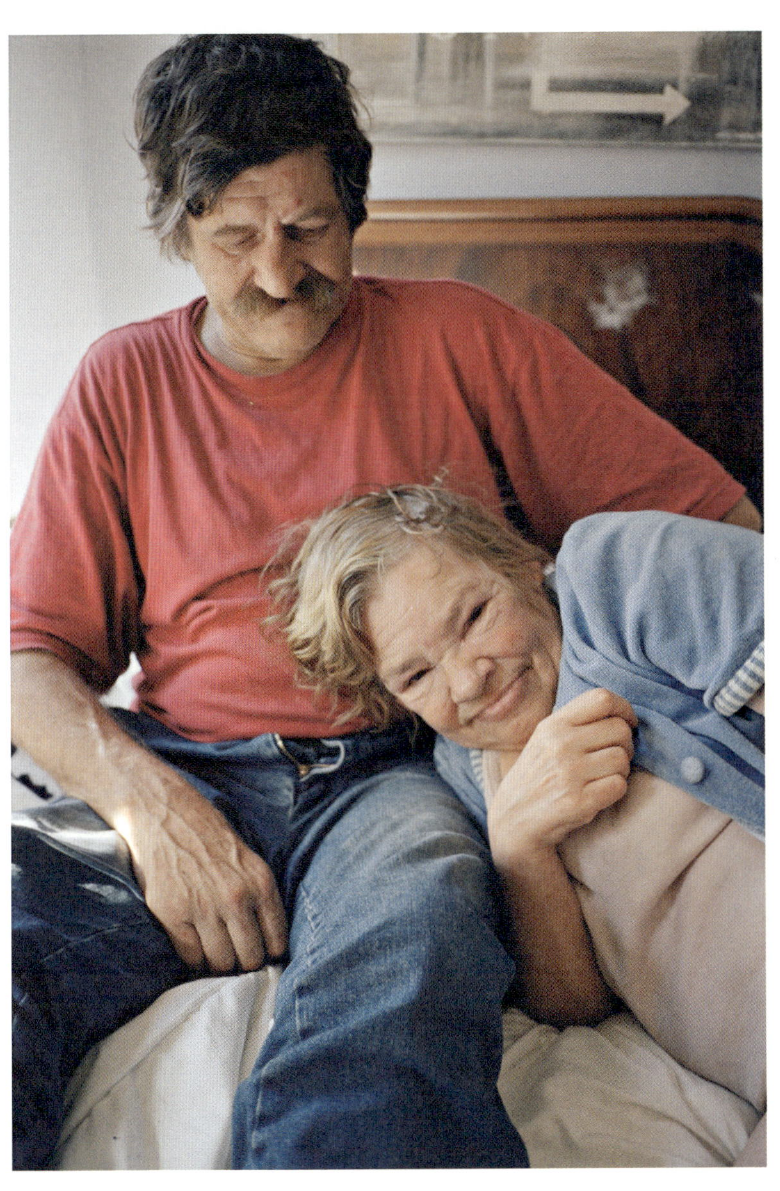

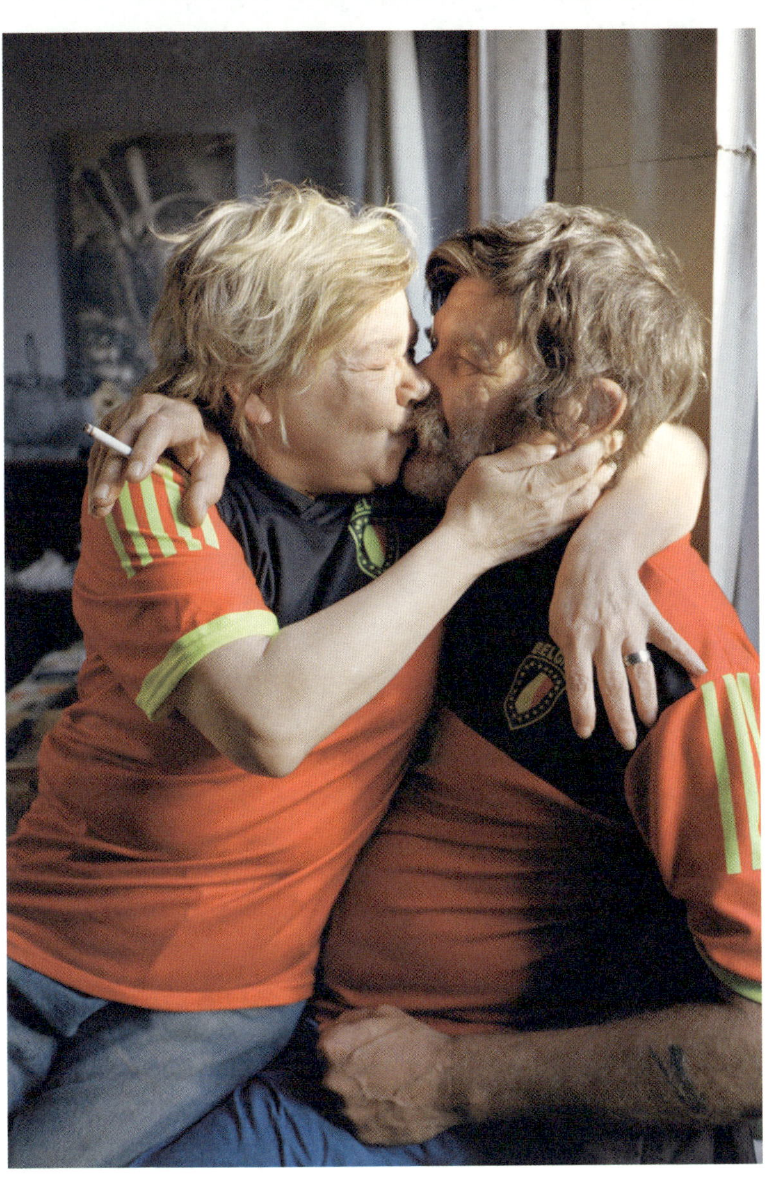

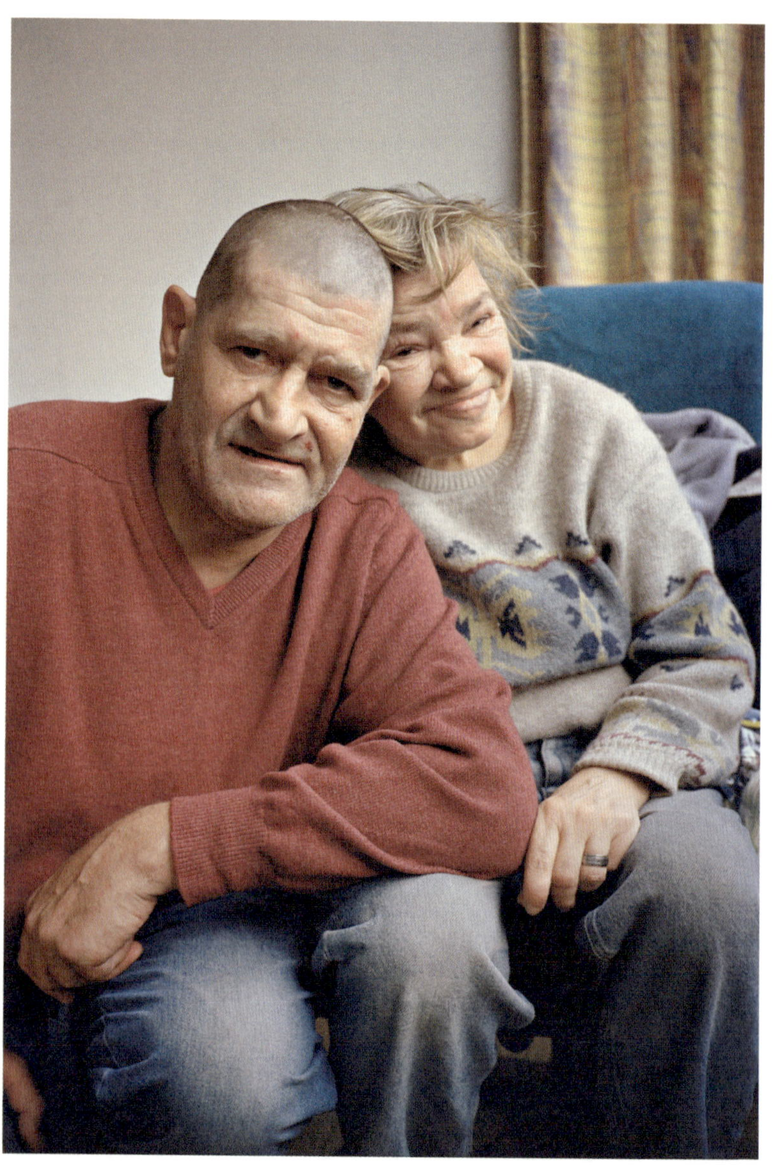

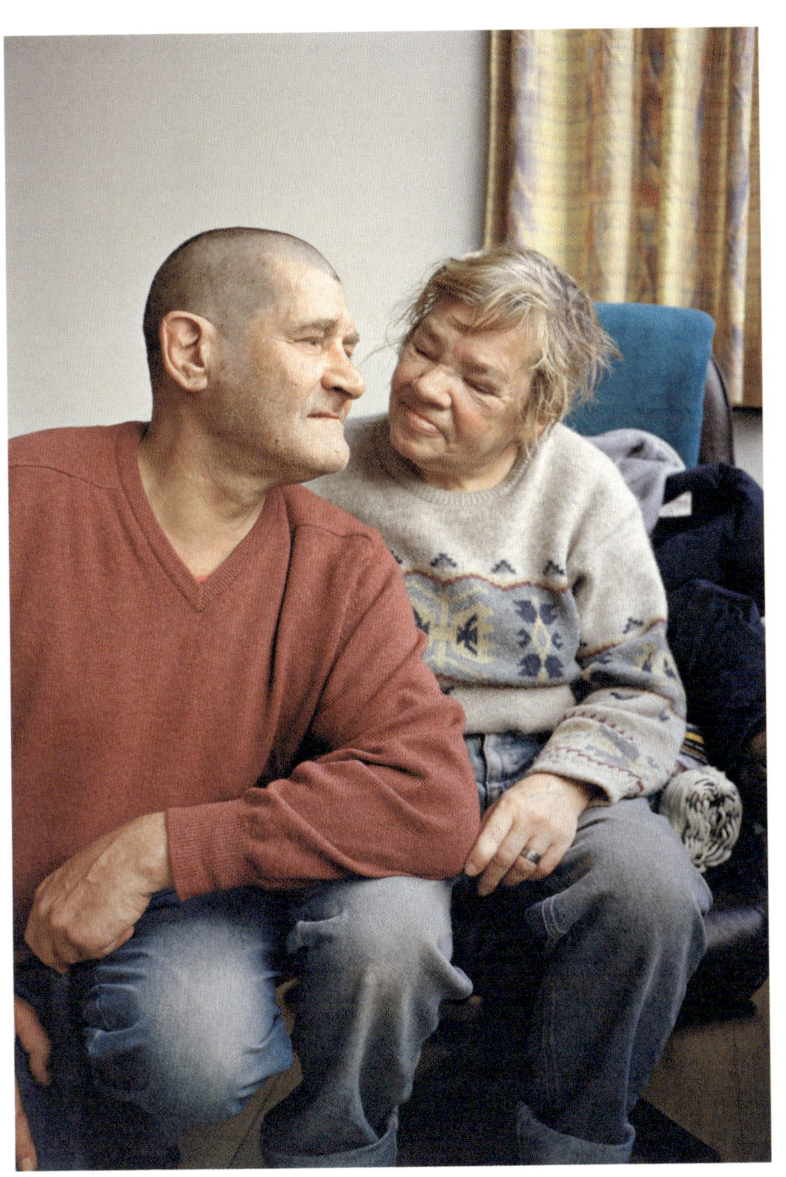

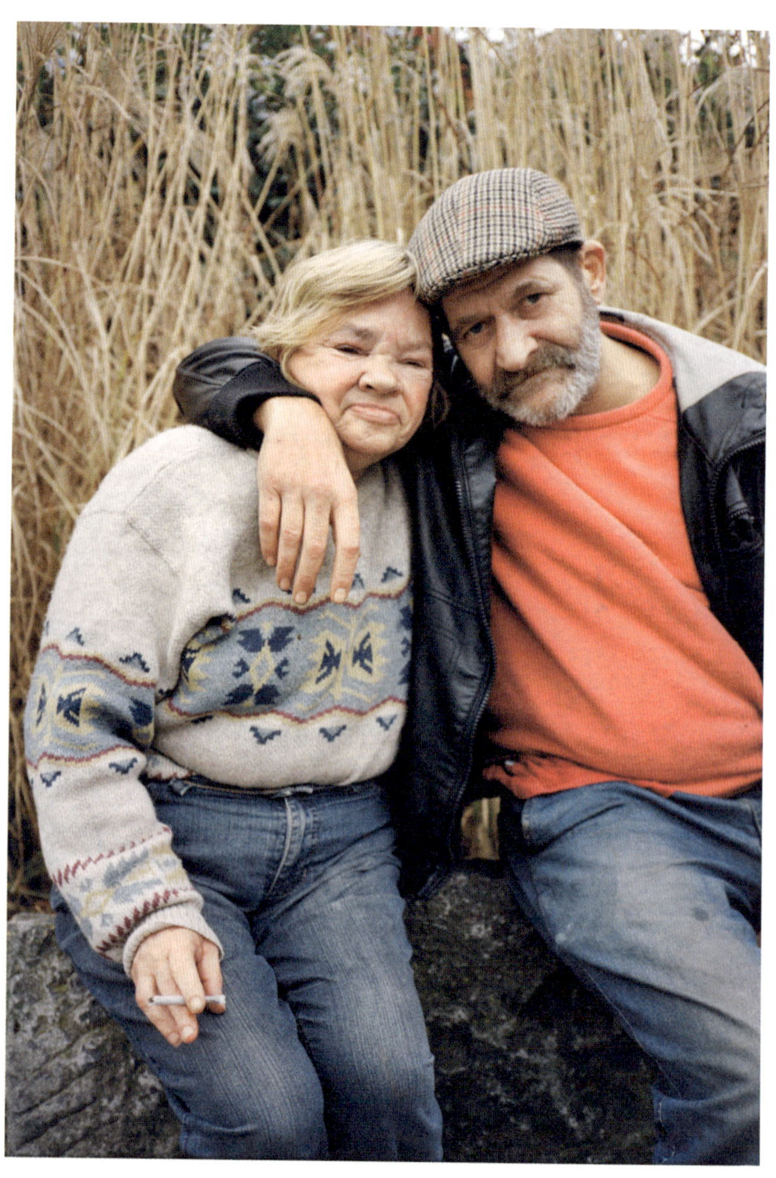

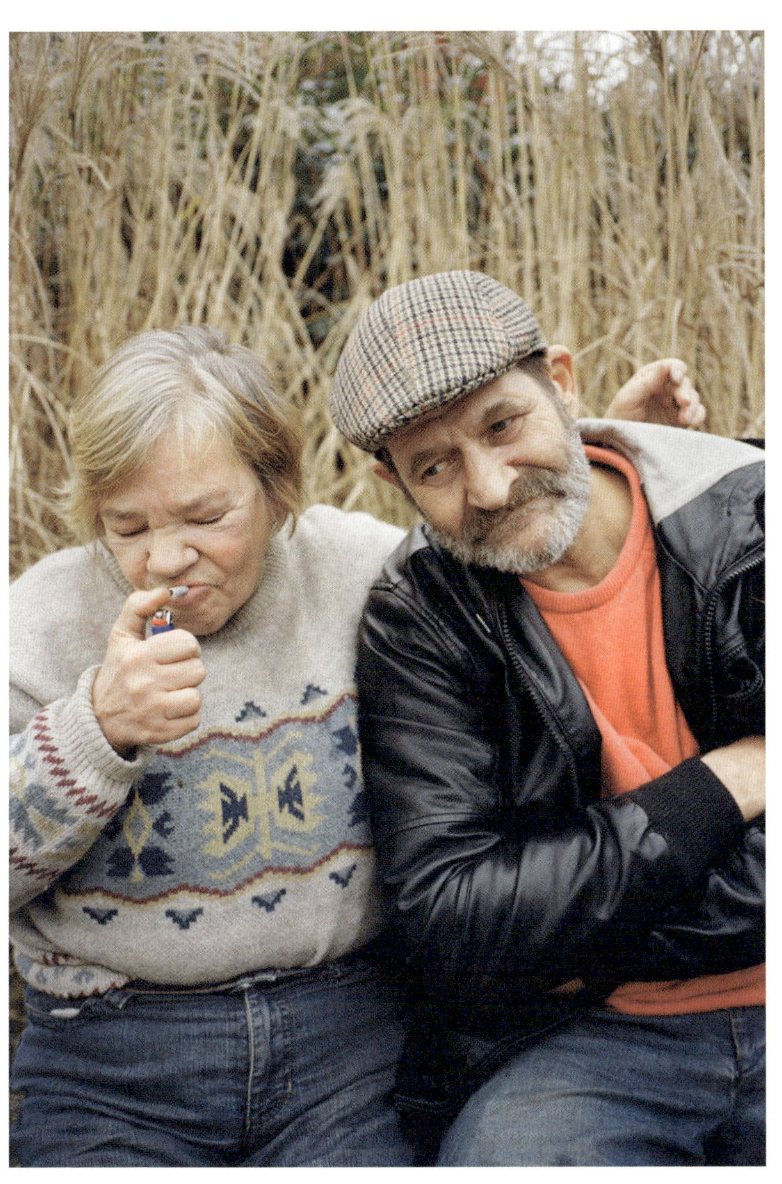

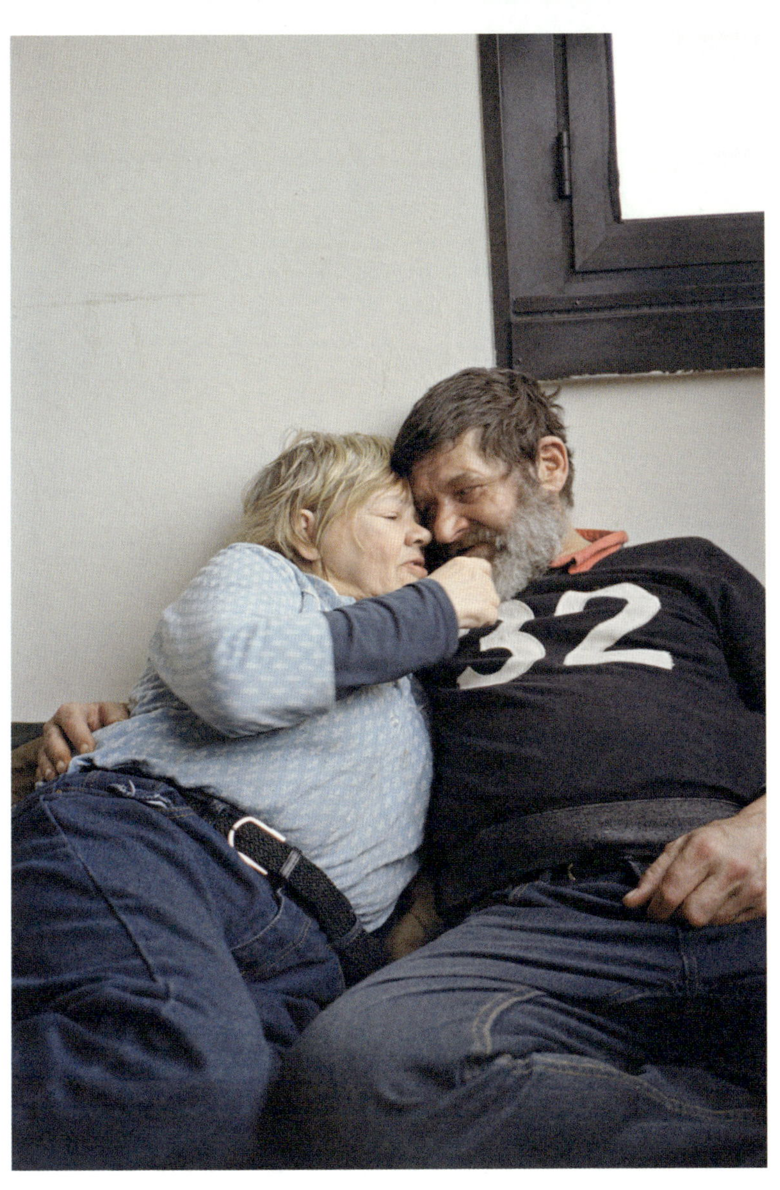

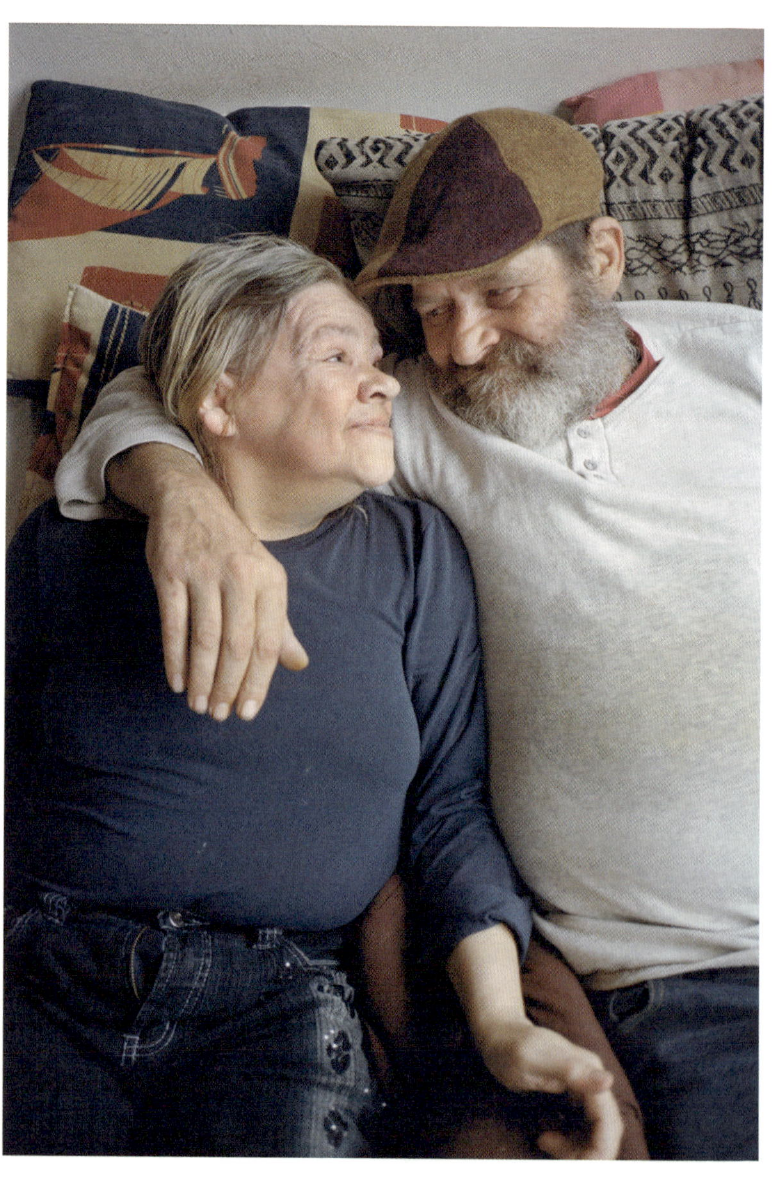

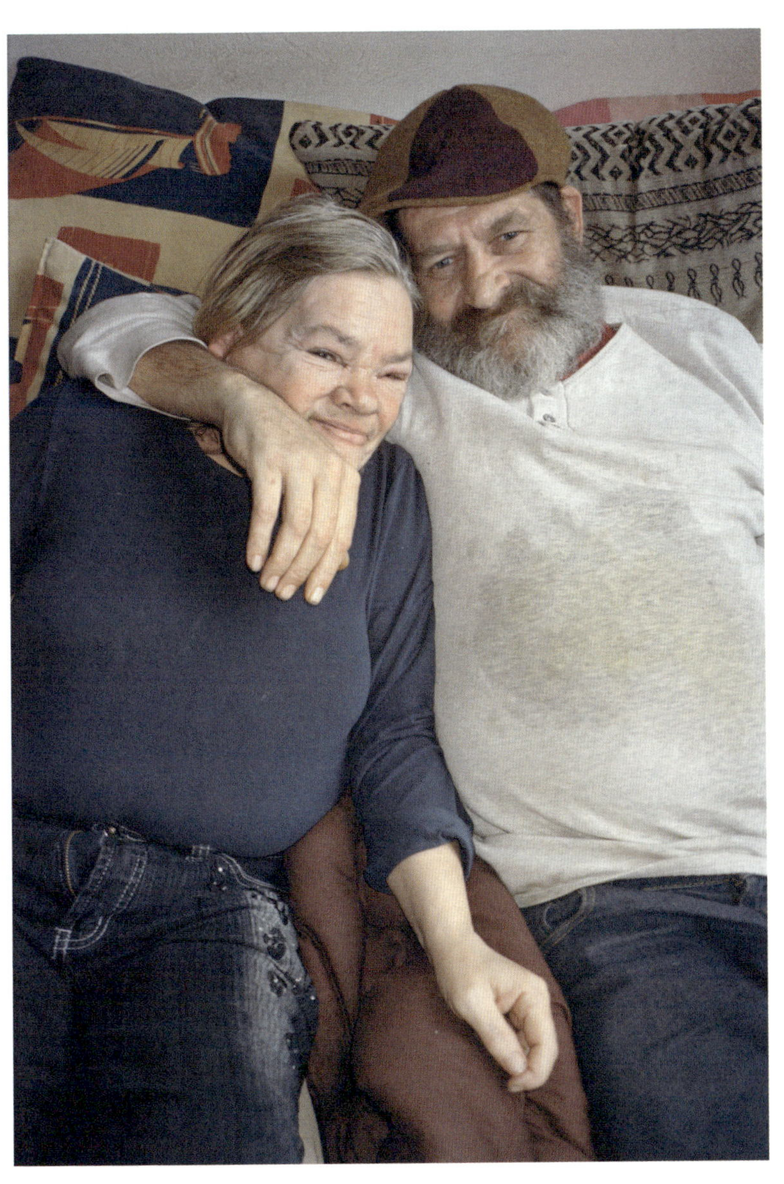

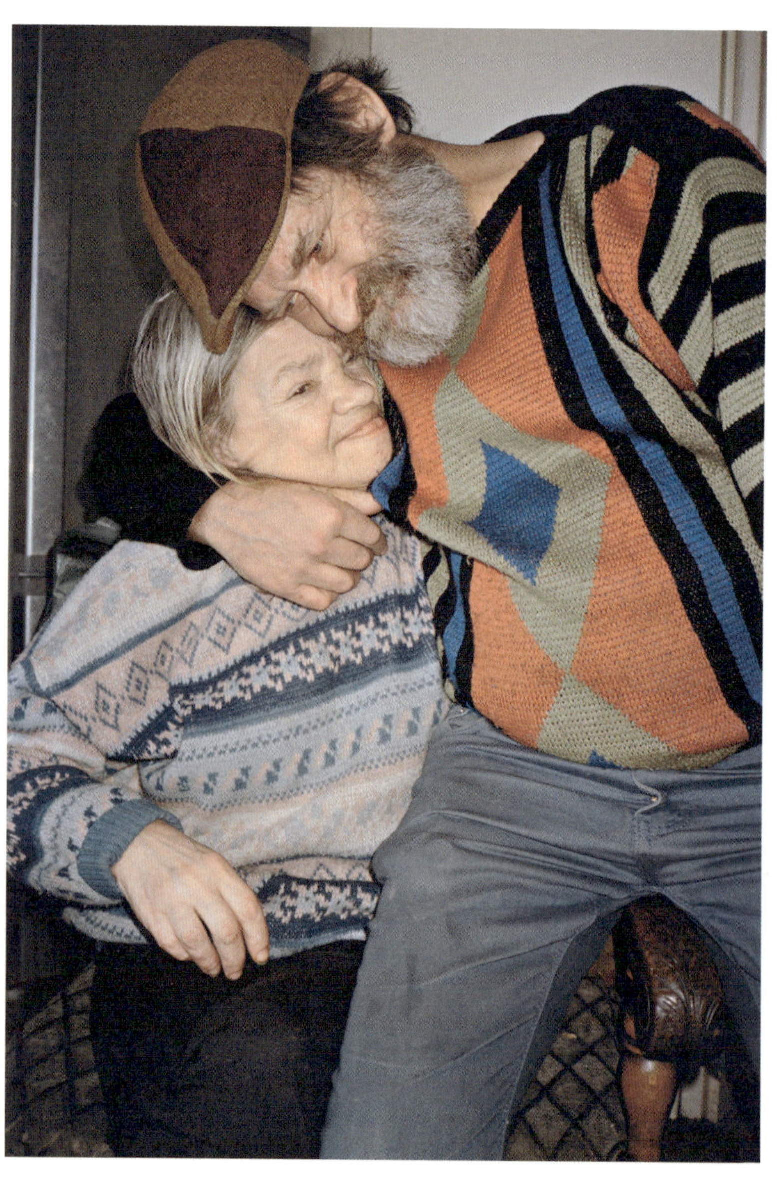

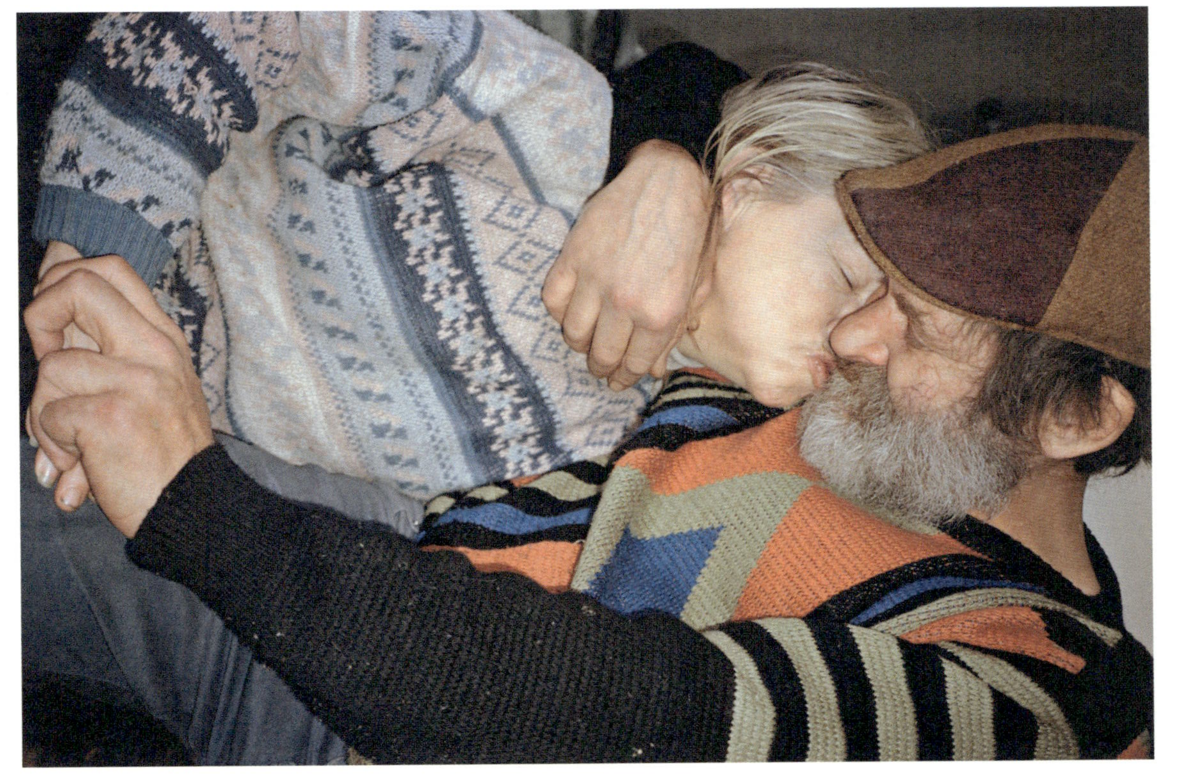

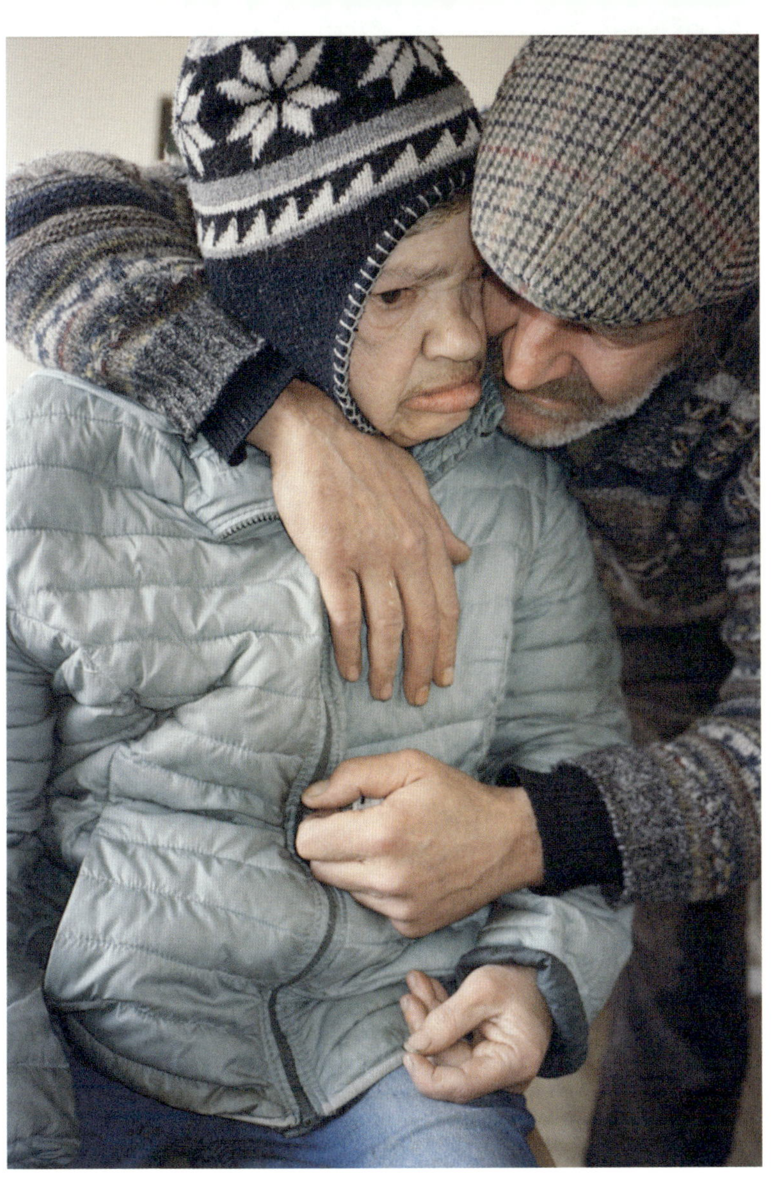

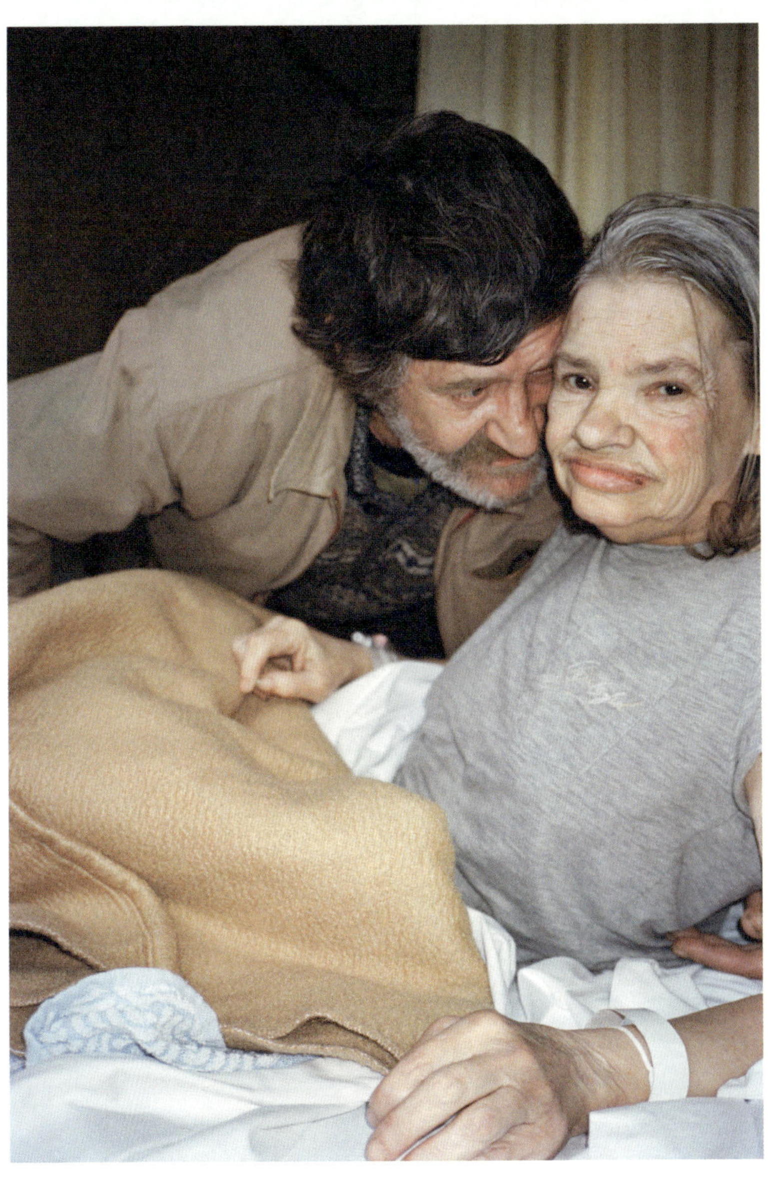

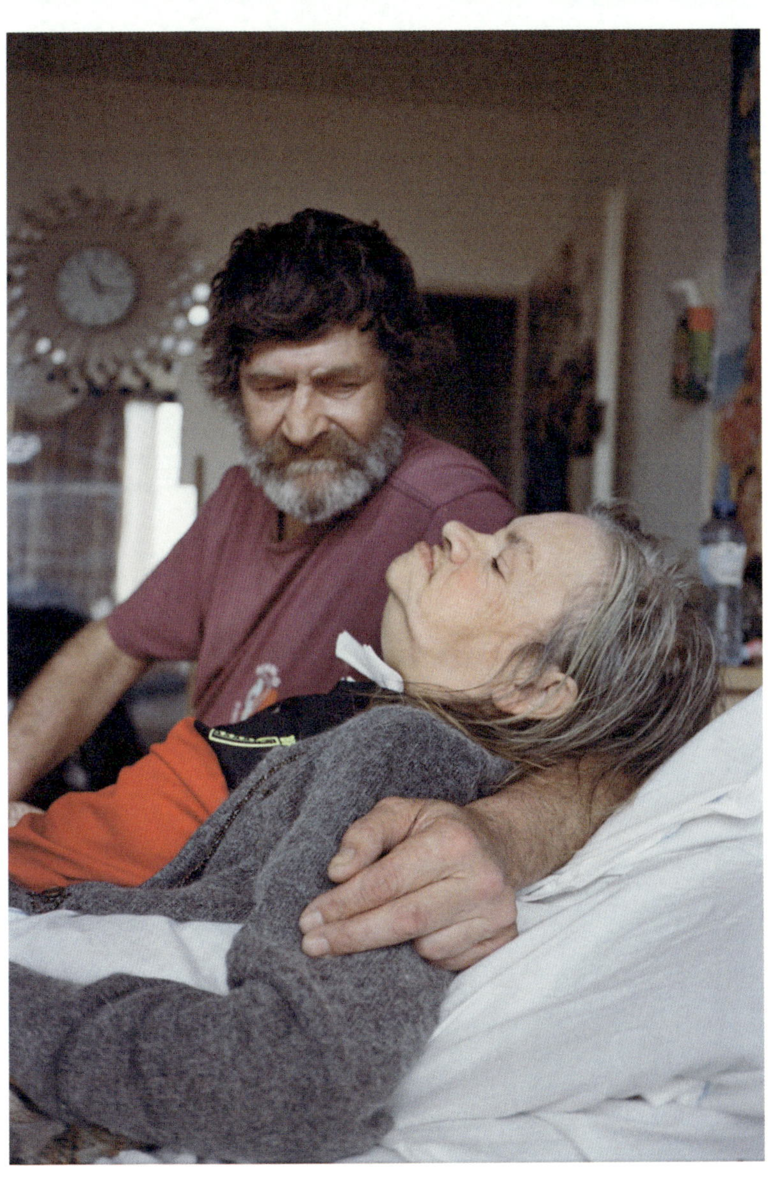

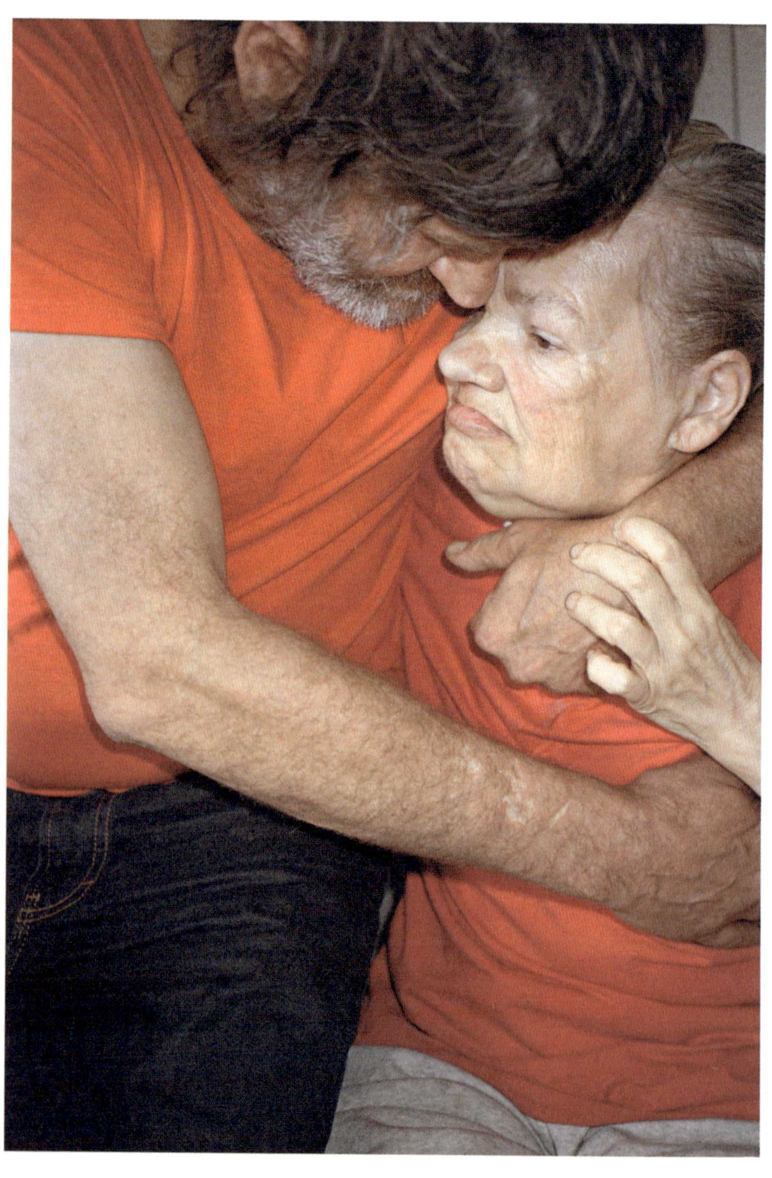

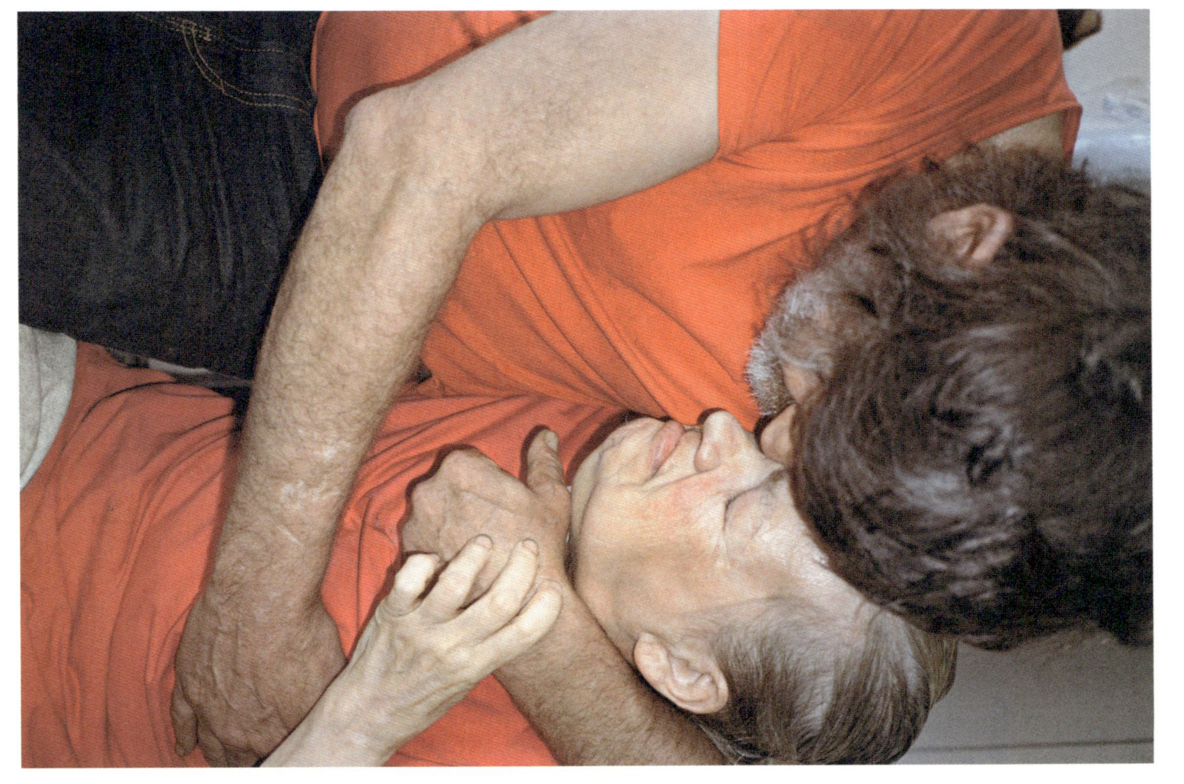

"I met Lilly when I was working at the Foire du Midi fair in Brussels," says Claude van Halen of his late partner, Liliane Maes. "I met her on the 14th of July 1995. The boss of a bar asked me, 'Claude do you want to go with her, because her man is beating her?' I said yes. I even left my job for her. I went with her and we stayed together for so long, for 23 years."

"We stayed together from the first day. It was love at first sight. She said, 'Claude I have to tell you—I cannot cook.' And then I said, 'No problem, I'm a butcher and I can cook for you.' The thing was she really loved to eat so I did cook for her. Maybe that's what made her strong. But even when Lilly was young, she was strong, even when her husband asked her to prostitute herself she said no and was able to fight back against him and beat him."

"I fell in love with her simplicity. She was not a woman who lived in luxury or wanted luxury. She never wore make up, there was no product on her face. She just said all the time, 'I have a problem. They are too little… (She meant her boobs)'… And I would say, 'It's not important. That's what God gave you.'"

"We lived on the streets in different places, in front of Pierrot rue des Fleuristes, then in my brother's place, the place where he committed suicide. After that we lived on the streets for more than 10 years on and off, but also in small flats until she got evicted. But we always found a new place in the end. We got by."

"The most romantic moment we had together was when we were in the woods in Rhode-Saint-Genèse close to Brussels where I grew up. The mayor of the town saw us making love. But luckily I knew her and she said 'just remember to take all your stuff with you.' And you know what? We forgot our underwear. Both of us. That's the truth."

Lilly passed away on June 6th 2018, Claude by her side till the end. The romance between them is kept alive through Vincen Beeckman's pictures of Claude and Lilly. They are pictures of love, small sequences of affection, of touching, holding, kissing and being together in each other's company.

"I met Vincen because of a picture he took at Brussels Central Station," says Claude. "It's my favourite, the one where Lilly is wearing the blue jacket. But I like them all and I remember all the places where he made them, and the times he made them, including the time on Lilly's birthday when Vincen brought us a bottle of champagne to celebrate."

That first picture shows Claude with his arms around Lilly in the blue jacket, then as the sequence progresses the hats change, the coats change, Claude's hair changes. Lilly puts her hand on Claude's leg, they both look at the camera, him in a sheepskin jacket, both looking at the camera. In the next picture, they've turned and kissed. They kiss for the camera but also for themselves, for the love that lives on through the memory. Claude grows a beard, he has his head shaved, they wear Belgium football shirts for the big match, they kiss, Claude wraps his arms around Lilly and Lilly wraps her arms around Claude, Claude strokes his beard, they kiss, they are in love. And then gradually Lilly fades away, she's sick, she falls into her bed, she falls into herself with Claude at her side, and so she passes.

The memories and Vincen's photographs are what remain but these are not the only pictures that Claude has of himself and Lilly. "One time Vincen gave us disposable cameras and five of my pictures were shown when he exhibited some images in a little exhibition. It was really nice; we had beer and shared some beautiful moments. But I have some pictures of Lilly and me from a disposable camera that I didn't give back to Vincen, that I don't want to show anybody. We are naked in them. We made some nude images and I went on my own to get the images at the photo shop. I told the person 'Don't look at that too much.'"

"I will never find another Lilly. That's why I want to go into an old people's home. I'm waiting for that to happen."

Lilly may be gone, but Claude still has his pictures and memories of the love and affection that helped them both make it through the hard times, times when the only warmth and comfort was that which came from the love they felt for each other.

"I was in love more and more each year," says Claude. "My love grew and grew, it never stopped."

Colin Pantall

APE #131
Vincen Beeckman
Claude & Lilly

ISBN 9789493146068
www.artpapereditions.org
www.vincenbeeckman.com
First print of 500 copies
March 2019

Graphic design: 6'56"
(www.6m56s.com)
Photography: Vincen Beeckman
Text: Colin Pantall
Printing: Wilco Art Books,
Amersfoort

Thanks to Claude et Lilly, Coraly Aliboni, Diogènes et Aline, Dupret Annabelle, Friling Charlotte et Cédric, Jacques Cerami, KZG Arnold et David, Le Château d'Eau Toulouse, ma famille et mes proches, Nicole and Olivier Gevaerts, Recyclart Art Center, Romario, Sylvia Cocozza, Bertrand Cavalier, Xuan Nativitas, Zinneke Parade.